Style Guide to Home Decor

& Furnishing

ARTPOWER

Style Guide to Home Decor & Furnishing

ARTPOWER

Publisher: Lu Jican
Publishing Director: Wang Yu
Chief Editor: Li Aihong
Executive Editors: Hu Ning, Li Juan
Art Designers: Chen Ting, Lan Meng

Registered Address
Suites 2001, 20/F., Chinachem Tower, 36 Connaught Road Central, Hong Kong, China
Tel: 852-31840676
Fax: 852-25432396

Editorial Department
G009, Floor 7th, Yimao Centre, Meiyuan Road, Luohu District, Shenzhen, China
Tel: 86-755-82913355
Fax: 86-755-82020029

Web: www.artpower.com.cn / www.acs.cn
Sales & Distribution: artpower@artpower.com.cn / overseasales@artpower.com.cn
Press & Editorial Submissions: press@artpower.com.cn / contact@artpower.com.cn

ISBN 978-988-18769-3-5

Printed and bound in China.

PREFACE

Soft Decor Design, the Soul of Space

"Soft Decor Design", this concept is put forward in comparison to the traditional "hard" design, which means all the movable, flexible, and replaceable elements in a space, such as furniture, lighting, home textile, decoration and ornaments, etc. If we say hard interior design is the skeleton of a space, soft design will be the soul of it. As the design industry blossoms, soft interior design gradually bourgeons with the public increasingly recognising it. "Light finishing, and heavy decoration", a saying we always refer to, greatly assures the significance of soft decor design.

In the recent years, the style of soft decor design tends to be more simple and succinct – materials, structures and colours are all simplified and streamlined. Besides, more people have started paying attention to Asian culture, while focusing on the details of history and culture, also requesting highly for quality and comfort of space. Surely, there are people pursuing more "personalised" or tailored space, with the "mix-and-match" way, creating distinctive icons to make their home absolutely unique.

I have always had affirmative votes for soft decor culturally. Soft decor design is, instead of the simple accumulation of products, the cultivation of some sort of aura, and where a certain life style begins. By refining the functions, such design enables people to live more comfortably and conveniently. Not just about purchasing products, an interior soft decor designer is required to have unique understandings on space design, rich product resources, and ability of selecting and matching all different soft interior elements, so that they can further optimise the design with the help of the concise cognition of the space, which is also a direct representation of the delight in life as well as the literacy in culture.

Soft decor design is a specialised skill and profession. If you would like to have more professional and in-depth understandings on this industry, I would recommend you to start from this book.

Jiang Xiaolin
Co-Direction Interior Design

CONTENTS

ADVANCED MINIMALISM

ADVANCED MINIMALISM

Simplicity Love

"From tomorrow on, I will be a happy man;

Grooming, chopping and traveling all over the world;

From tomorrow on, I will care about foodstuff and vegetable,

living in a house towards the sea with spring blossoms."

Does Haizi's poem intrigue you? Using the burning preference and passion to avoid the hustle and bustle of city life, and choosing a romantic coast to live. Seeing the ebb and flow every day and experiencing the ups and downs of mood. Let the sunshine fill the room, and decorate it with odd-shaped shells and freshly picked buds, delicate glass bottles and jars, a coir carpet and coverings hand-made with white cotton and linen fabric. Carefully preparing a delicious meal, just like the poem — "skillfully mincing meat as smooth as snow, with brilliant seasoning making the dishes as crowd-pleaser", cooking with gratitude towards the person and the ingredients, and by doing so, you could create the slow life of your own. Changes in life can be easily made when taking on a different perspective to it, the whole world begins to change once you look at it differently, like the mindset described in Haizi's poem — I face the sea, with flowers blossoming in the spring breeze.

Some say happiness is money that can't be used up, and being able to laugh everyday; some say happiness is when the boss allows you to have a few paid days off. Obviously, the former rises from the lack of money, while the later comes from the lack of time. But when you have enough life experiences, money and time, you would realize that, happiness is simple – slow down your pace and live on the basis of life, simplicity is the best, and that's how life should be, simple and warm with some occasional surprises.

Wonder if you have such experience – In a slightly humid but comfortable afternoon, you take a glimpse into the wall corner and find a small handful of weed just grow out of it, they are still fresh and soft, "should I get rid of them", you think, but you then hesitate: "that is a life, a new-born life, I should leave it be". And with changing seasons, they are getting greener and stronger. When the winter comes, you get worried and see if they get frozen, upon your touch, although feeling a bit dry, they are soft and still standing against the cold and waiting for the coming year, when they could thrive.

To some extent, our life is similar to those weeds — we can't choose where we come from as well as the unpredictable toughness along the way, the only thing we could determine is the way we live our life, we better keep our head down, get our hands dirty and focus and stop complaining, learn the necessary skills, and that's it, keep your life simple, instead of worrying and shouldering too much pressure and desires. It may be hard to make our life easier, but we can always make it simpler by keeping a clear vision on your true goal and doing the necessary things to achieve it. So, keep going, keep your life simple.

Simplified but not simple, life back to its nature.

IMAGE © GLOBAL VIEWS

IMAGE © GLOBAL VIEWS

Advanced Minimalism Proposition

Minimalism comes from Western Modernism in the early 20th century, its founder is Walter Gropius. To promote function as the first principle, Gropius made furniture modeling fit for the production line. To promote minimalism in the architectural decoration, it simplified them including the design elements colors, lighting, raw materials to a minimum extent which improved the requirements of colors and material texture. It tried to achieve decorative effect of doing more with less. Minimalism developed on fundamental of rebellion against the trend of retro and Minimalist aesthetics in the mid-80s, and began to integrate into the field of interior design in the early 90s. This simple form of expression meets the needs of people. For example, emotional, instinctive and rational needs of space environment. It is gradually being the concern of the international community today.

Minimalism is not simple. It derived from careful consideration and innovation, rather simply "pile up" or "placed." Concise but not simple, it could be the best portrayal of modern minimalist style. No more decoration, it pays attention to modest proportion of modeling, emphasizing bright appearance, simple lines and functional design, and color in strong contrast or elegant pleasure. It reflects the modern fast-paced, simple and practical, but vibrant life. Because of the simple line and less decorative elements, modern style furniture needs the perfect soft decoration, in order to show beauty. Accessories in modern minimalist style are the most eclectic. Some ornaments with simple lines, unique design and even very creative and personalized style may be treated as modern minimalist.

Characteristic

Minimalism emphasizes practicality. It also stresses the individuation and abstraction of indoor space form and component, and pursues the depth and precision of material, technology and space, and reflects the concise and bright sense of times and abstract beauty.

Lines

Minimalism often uses geometric structure, composited of curve and asymmetric lines. Some lines are soft and elegant, and some vigorous and full of sense of rhythm. The whole three-dimensional form integrates into methodical, rhythmic curves. The use of simple structure and beautiful shape brings pleasure and leisure, which is the pursuit of a modern psychological comfort.

Pattern

Walls, railings, window frames and furniture are with such pedicels, buds, vines, insect wings and a variety of natural beauty, wavy shape patterns. Compared with the traditional style, modern minimalism with the most straightforward decorative language clarifies the home space to create the atmosphere, and then gives the space personality and calmness, but also presents the avant-garde, unfettered feeling.

Color

Minimalism avoids complex color scheme but different from the absolute black and white, it stands out in an implicit way. To achieve that, it requires a simplified colour selection from colours of similar shapes, or the ones in contrast.

Material

The quality and texture of Minimalist deco is the new luxury. Instead of those strong and aggressive use of lines and materials, the modern Minimalism takes on materials like steel grass, stainless steel. Also, traditional craftsmanship is involved, the use of crafted glass, ceramic and iron work in their pure and elegant forms, adding a sense of art to your space.

1

GLOBAL VIEWS

IMAGE © GLOBAL VIEWS

This clam but not boring space takes large white area as backdrop, which is enriched with furniture and accessories of gold colour and various shapes of beige.

The corner of living room chooses warm colored wood as main material. Wall painting and desk decorations have become the focus.

1.1 LIVING ROOM

IMAGE © GLOBAL VIEWS

IMAGE © GLOBAL VIEWS

IMAGE © GLOBAL VIEWS

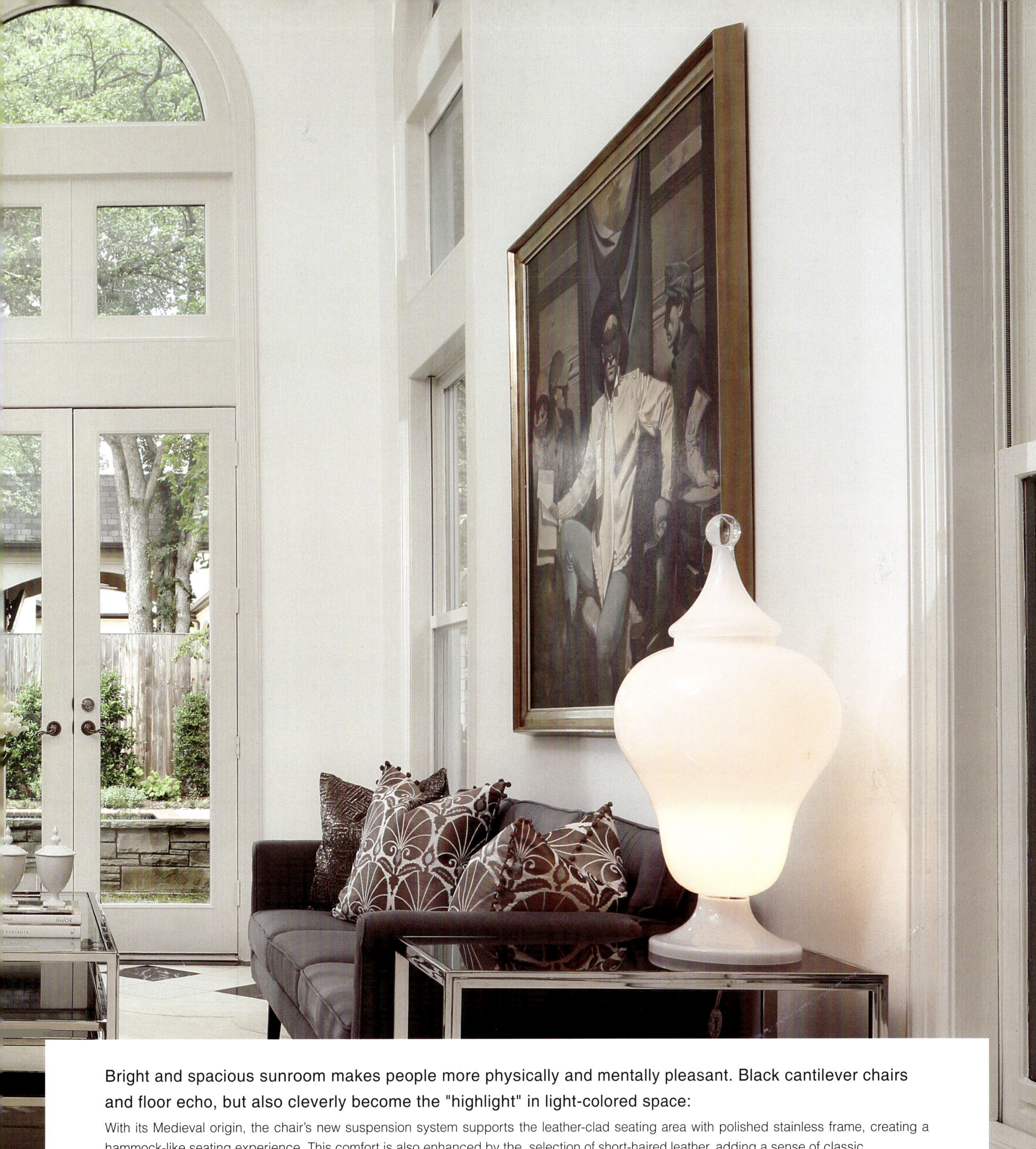

Bright and spacious sunroom makes people more physically and mentally pleasant. Black cantilever chairs and floor echo, but also cleverly become the "highlight" in light-colored space:

With its Medieval origin, the chair's new suspension system supports the leather-clad seating area with polished stainless frame, creating a hammock-like seating experience. This comfort is also enhanced by the selection of short-haired leather, adding a sense of classic.

Decorated by black branches, the cabinet feels calm with a sense of design. And with red coral pattern carpet and bright-colored accessories, the overall colors are lively and full of passion.

For color selection, white, ivory and grey tone colors are widely used across the space with blue and green as embellishment, highlighting a sense of tradition and elegance.

The living room is mainly in golden yellow, including the tea table and side table, making the whole room bright. The lamping bracket is fully covered by fan-shaped brass leaves, and its branch-shaped appearance adds a little fun to its classical style. The cocktail table in the living room center is also unusual, with the smooth dumb white marble table and four long spike-like table legs, while the two extended nails that link across four corners making the table more stable. The small tea table next to the sofa is extraordinary, which is surrounded by the steel branches in casual. Braches are also intertwined by themselves, supporting the dumb white marble table. The entire appearance makes people thinking of a pair of tango dancers.

The colors of furniture such as carpet, sofa and pillow are harmonious and vivid. There is no lack of stability in the changes, and the scenery outside the windows has become indispensable embellishment in the space.

1.2 DINING ROOM

With brown as the main color of restaurant, the clever use of similar color scale, and elegant green planting flowers, make the living room both decent and elegant.

The leaves will reflect the warmth of the golden glory, when the light is lit. The jagged dining table is inspired by Global Views' best-selling products-Serrated Wall Table. The zebra-like woodwork looks like a chessboard. The jagged base acts like an accordion. More specifically, the table itself is two layers, can be opened on both sides, after the extension can accommodate 12 people dining at the same time.

The dining room above uses brown as main color. To add a bit of lightness to the room colored with brown, lively shape and glass material are added to its furniture — the dining table with transparent glass top and flower-shaped base matched with a few U-shaped glass candlesticks; The wall-sided Geneva glass cabinet, framed by American white oak, has 3 transparent glass sides, and the four glass panels inside can be rearranged to suit your display need, with the mirror back and the built-in lighting, the cabinet is ideal for showcasing your favourite collection.

1.3 STUDY ROOM

The study is elegant and ivory white-based, with carpets, cushions and decorative flowers to increase the temperature. Hollow decorative desk is mainly made of broadleaf hardwood, and there are very exotic zebra decorative panel, auburn surface coated with varnish and hand-waxed as a protective layer. The desk is equipped with a large drawer for stationery, such as pencils, adding functionality to its design.

A muted and neutral color scheme is used for the study below — the white and ivory used in the the furniture and decoration match well with that of the tricolour flower-patterned wallpaper. The heavily brown-colored desk is lightened by the transparency of crystal bulb-shaped base of the desk lamp, and together they become the special feature of the study. The curved lines and texture of the silk lampshade also help to soften the image of the space.

The bedroom is painted by a warm color, yellow. Both bedding and lamp are designed to fit with the owner's comfortable sleep. The classical and innovative lamp can be described as a highlight of the bedroom. This lamp has a solid brass and vase shape body, with the quadrate pedestal made by enamel iron. Its body was twined by flowers, creeping to the top. The lampshade is also in bronze, aiming to be consistent with the body, due to the wonderful combination between the elegant bronze and classic black. Besides, the collocation by the rounded lampshade and angular square is decent.

1.4 BEDROOM

To help relax, a wide range of warm orange tone colors are applied to the bedroom. The bathroom is connected to the bedroom, and designer is bold to keep the two walls of the floor to ceiling windows. Concise and neat style bathtub was placed by the window. The owner can enjoy the views outside while bathing. The sculpture like two arms staying together is a stool made of Portuguese reinforced ceramic, the two open hands may look fun but also provide comfortable seating. The craftsmanship involved makes it an artwork standing alone, or you could follow the photo on the right, using it to hold your toiletries, and that works brilliantly.

IMAGE © GLOBAL VIEWS

1.5 PRODUCT DISPLAY

IMAGE © GLOBAL VIEWS

DwellStudio Designers Collection

02 Golden Palm Leaf Mirror

The palm-leaf-formed mirror frame is crafted with iron, on which there is shinny golden paint.

01 Malachite Pattern Decorative Plate

Malachite pattern decorative plate is made of flown glass with malachite pattern. Standing alone, it's stunning enough, whether used for decoration or as a tableware.

03 Brass Branches White Marble Tray — Large / Small

Solid brass is carved into a branch shape, mounted on a white natural marble plate. The dazzling handles, together with the marble plate, form a lovely chic tray.

04 Silhouette Figure Table Lamp

Colored with fresh and elegant tones, the lamp takes Portugal-made ceramic portrait figure as lamp body, transparent glass base and grey nickel-plated lampshade.

05 Light Blue Chamomile Ceramic Jar — Large / Small

The shape is classical. It is also functional. Beautiful light blue active glaze is soft and fresh.

06 Olive Green Carambola Bowl

The carambola bowls have elegant lines and fine details, which are used to pay tribute to a long-history and exquisite-craft Portuguese ceramic. When placed alone, it is a unique decoration; After putting fruits in, it turns into a beautiful artistic fruit plate.

08 Matt White Carambola Box

The carambola series have elegant lines and fine details, which are used to pay tribute to a long-history and exquisite-craft Portuguese ceramic.

07 Babylon Floor Lamp

Taking the same central axis, a number of circular parts stacking up and down to form the lampshade of this floor lamp, the symmetrical design resembles the legendary tower standing wildly in field.

09 The White Marble Spike Table

With a golden appearance and white marble desktop, it is elegant. Three iron spike-type table foots are in simple line, making the table solid and stable.

10 Ivory Wayne Chair

Its erected high back, with handrails at the convergence of the smooth arc, and thick cushion, mean that every detail regards to the comfort of experience. With walnut chain legs, medieval wind is blowing.

11 Black / Ivory Wood Pallet

It uses medium density fiberboard as the main body. Its surface is cocoa wood decorated with varnish. Two small trays can be embedded in the large tray. Concise lines and the classic shape are never out of date.

13 Aluminum White Vase — Large / Medium / Small

Aluminum vase presents silver plated appearance. It shows fresh taste when plugs a few branches of calla.

12 White Leather Box With Handle

Full leather package and handle with nickel-plated stainless steel are noble and refined. Box body with linen lining, is your favorite collection for valuables.

15 Copper Mesh Glass Vase — Large / Medium / Small

Glass vase with double-layer structure, is very strong in fact. In addition to metallic color dot-like texture at inner, it is inlaid with real metal debris. The combination of them forms incredible texture.

14 Blue Amoeba Glass Bowl — Large / Small

Early porcelain became the source of inspiration for the glass bowl. The landslide effect of the flown glass made it a unique shape, and especially the amoeba pattern made it even more unique. The product has passed through the food safety test, which is not only a decoration, but also chic tableware.

OMENIA

IMAGE © OMENIA

Fashion

2.1 LIVING ROOM

IMAGE © OMENIA

The colors of metal furniture grey walls and brown wood flooring are harmonious, and also enhance the sense of dynamic space.

IMAGE © OMENIA

Orange, brown and wood color, these warm colors help heat up the space from the visual. Abstract pattern of painting as a decoration makes up the wall of emptiness. Schema and tone are based on the main home style, to create a consistent indoor atmosphere.

IMAGE © OMENIA

There is light, bright wide space, and full of color, with rich patterns. There is temperature and reminiscent. Matching with cotton wool carpets and other objects, metal furniture has rich texture and its cold smell of the metal itself is balanced.

IMAGE © OMENIA

2.2 HALLWAY DISPLAY

The color of metal furniture with black walls and brown wood flooring is harmonious, and also enhances the sense of dynamic space.

ROCKY

2.3 PRODUCT DISPLAY

IMAGE © OMENIA

Stainless Steel Vase

Streamlined stainless steel vase as a modern flower arrangement is popular in modern floriculture. In the daily modern style home furnishings, stainless steel vases and flowers are mixed to present a modern atmosphere and balanced texture creating a good decorative effect.

01 Chess

A wise man always knows his place on the chessboard of life. And despite the hustle and bustle in our life, there is so much more we could celebrate and feel, like having a glorious victory in a chess game. Taking that spirit, this furniture collection is tailored to bring sculpture art into our daily life.

02 Letter Vase

Modern people want their home to be more casual and relaxing. Free combination of letters series vases, will be able to meet your simple feelings for nature. Comfortable natural letters, you can always find out your favorite type, whether decorating at home or office, it is more than a ray of concise fashion charm.

03 Star Series

Gorgeous space is filled with demure and beautiful atmosphere. Concise light beads create a taste of life. Life should be so free. Looking at the quiet sky and recalling the past , you appreciate fine arts like jewelry, which touches you and makes you appreciate them meticulously.

04 Wine Set

The plain wine set and its elegant style bring us the visual enjoyment as well as the temperament improvement. You can be enthusiastic like fire, and also cherish the memorable history and stories. The wine set expresses a noble life style, which is perfectly matched with the mellow wine, directly touching you by heart.

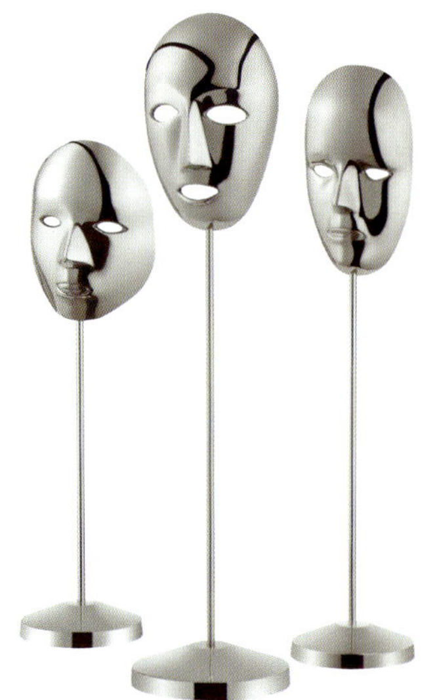

05 Sculpture Decoration

Time flies, recalling the past. After the vicissitudes, with a new attitude, it turns your wonderful memories into vivid reproduction, like magic and mottled "cross-time journey." And the difference is that all breakthroughs are condensed here.

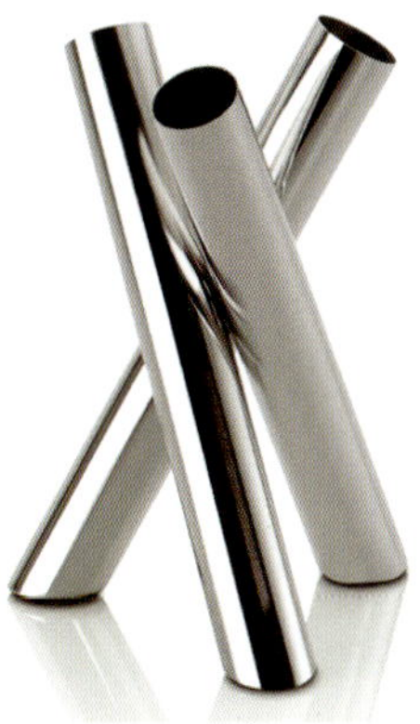

07 Bird Ornaments

There are abstract modeling, smart gesture. Stainless steel silver and champagne gold perfectly match, and enrich beauty of sculpture. The ornaments fit Omenia's concept of drawing materials from the nature. Displaying in the living room or study makes space more dynamic.

06 Round Tube Series

Simple geometric tubes are arranged in a patchwork, giving unlimited reverie. Plain shape always makes people can't help giving more glances. Ordinary things are also true — the more ordinary, the more interesting. It presents poetic space for people who love life and increases the green sense in display space.

08 Flower Container

Flower container full of metal smell brings out the characteristics most vividly, making people addictive. The concept of creating everything according to law of the nature is introduced into living room, which brought us aesthetics of life. "See a world in a grain of sand, and a heaven in a wild flower." A cluster of green and touch of sweet can burst into a different kind of home style.

10 Candlestick

In a quiet art space, everything has been attached to the natural mysterious power. The elegant candlelight and the tender texture from stainless steel, concisely and gracefully make the whole space comfortable and perfect. Faced with the transformation of the four seasons, the room is integrating into the natural and pristine atmosphere. And the elegant life style shows the deep appreciation of life.

09 Fruit Plate

The entire space is filled with orderly space and the rich atmosphere of stainless steel, for the real flavor of life in them. The fruit plate's style comes from its own texture, shape, complemented by exquisite ingredients. Several blooming flowers for leisure create a different atmosphere. The pleasure mood is even more joyful.

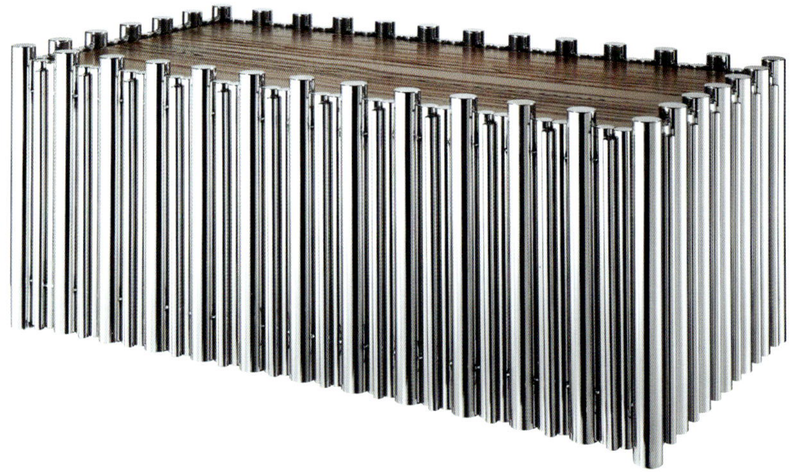

11 Hypericum Tea Table
Size | 1080mm × 560mm × 420mm

12 Hypericum Decoration
Size | 440mm × 125mm × 520mm

13 Lotus Leaf Decoration
Size | 500mm×210mm×400mm

14 Sail Decoration
Size | 580mm×200mm×1000mm

15 Windmill
Size | 385mm×130mm×360mm

16 Decoration of the Violin
Size | 240mm×85mm×635mm

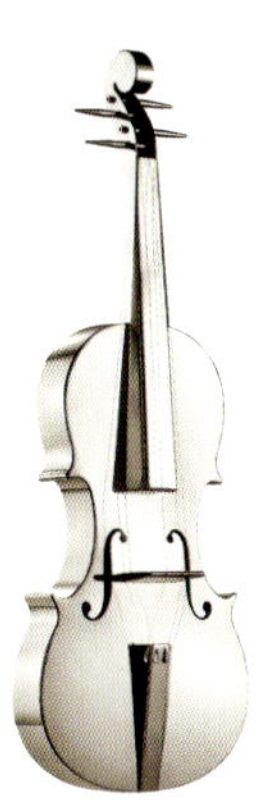

17 Champaign-Gold Rhombus Decoration
Size | 705mm×470mm×810mm

18 Dancing Butterflies Decoration
Size | 550mm × 300mm × 830mm

19 Ball Pile Decoration
Size | 400mm × 360mm × 640mm

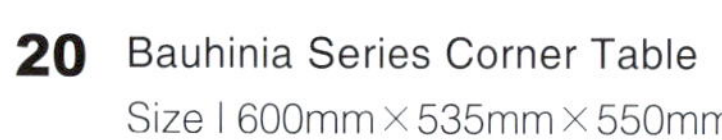

20 Bauhinia Series Corner Table
Size | 600mm × 535mm × 550mm

21 Countless Ties Decoration 1
Size | 415mm × 275mm × 530mm

22 Bauhinia Series Tea Table
Size | 1240mm × 800mm × 420mm

24 Lagerstroemia Tea Table
Size I 1235mm×605mm×430mm

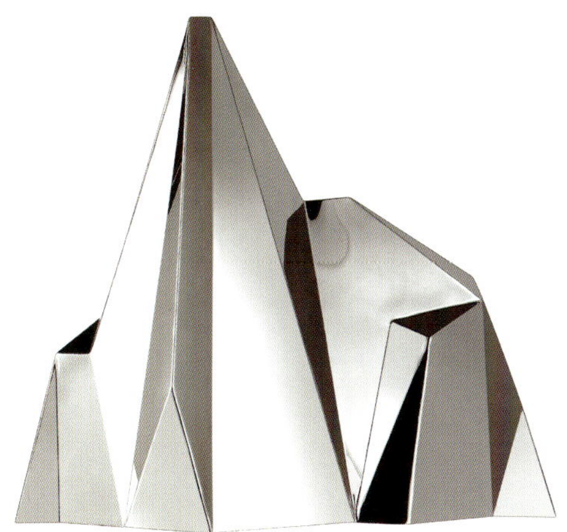

23 Rockery Decoration
Size I 700mm×330mm×600mm

25 Lagerstroemia Corner Table
Size I 570mm×570mm×600mm

26 A Great Hawk Spreading Its Wings
Size I 960mm×300mm×620mm

27 Champaign-Gold Pentacyclic Ring Decoration
Size I 450mm×210mm×500mm

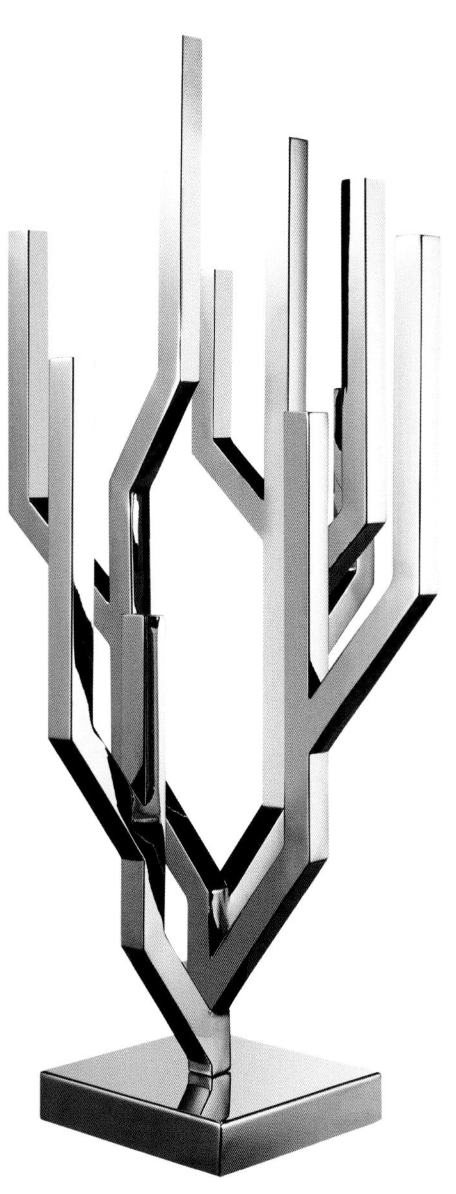

28 Yellow Chrysanthemum Decoration
Size | 335mm × 285mm × 640mm

29 Branches Corner Table
Size I 500mm × 500mm × 575mm

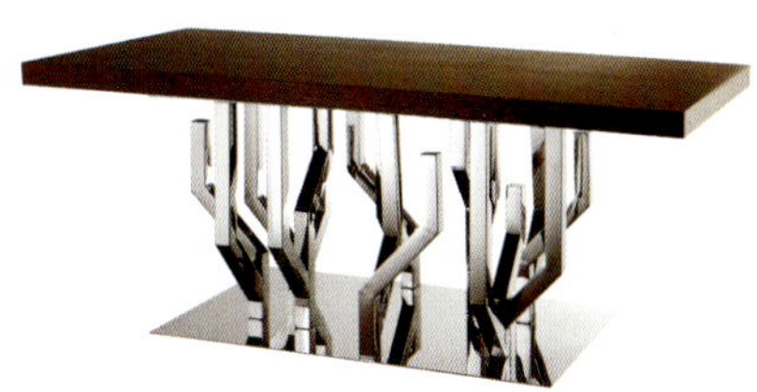

30 Branches Tea Table
Size I 1200mm × 600mm × 460mm

31 Round Tube Corner Table
Size I 700mm × 630mm × 460mm

32 Cottonrose-inspired Hallway Display
Size I 1500mm × 500mm × 795mm

33 Woven Wine Rack
Size I 500mm × 150mm × 265mm

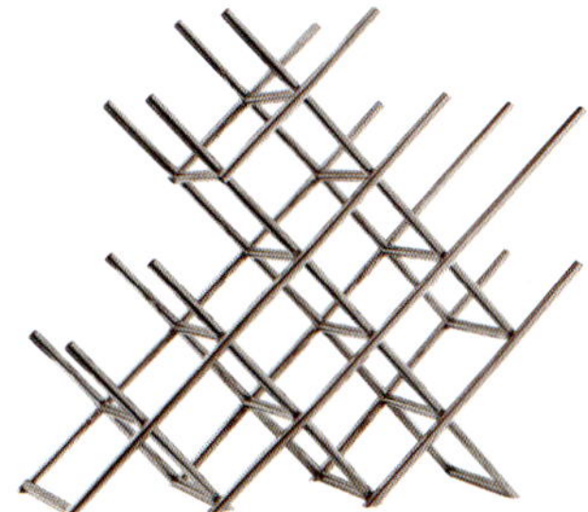

34 Woven Wine Rack
Size I 455mm × 160mm × 390mm

3

WELAND

IMAGE © WELAND

IMAGE © WELAND

TURKS IN EUROPE
TURKS IN EUROPE
TURKS IN EUROPE

3.1 LIVING ROOM

IMAGE © WELAND

The main colors are premium grey and bright yellow, so that the overall space does not seem boring. The room is decorated by geometric shapes, like carpet, furniture lines, pendants. Bonded with the delicate household products, the space looks concise with a sense of hierarchy.

To present a fresh and concise style, it uses white as the main color, combined with bright yellow carpet and a few orange flowers as a decoration as well as silver crystal furniture.

IMAGE © WELAND

Steady dark wood furniture and gray cloth carpet create a quiet atmosphere. The golden home accessories balance the colors and heighten atmosphere.

IMAGE © WELAND

IMAGE © WELAND

Dark sofa carpet and, metal furniture and jewelry match with each other. Their texture is balanced, without a sense of dullness.

IMAGE © WELAND

Restaurant with orange-based colors, beige wallpaper, and silver and copper furniture, has a deep sense of warmth.

3.2 DINING ROOM

IMAGE © WELAND

3.3 BEDROOM

The color of the bedroom furniture is mainly in blue, but due to the wooden materials, it does not bring out a sense of coldness. The wallpaper is in blue-green, echoed with the furniture, and the texture is also in geometric shape. The elegant color is matched with the copper jewelry, which let us feel like spring, making the whole space more vivid.

IMAGE © WELAND

3.4 PRODUCT DISPLAY

IMAGE © WELAND

01 Hang Decoration | 60cm×3.5cm

02 Bookend | 34cm×8cm×27cm

03 Animal Decoration | 11cm×4cm×6cm

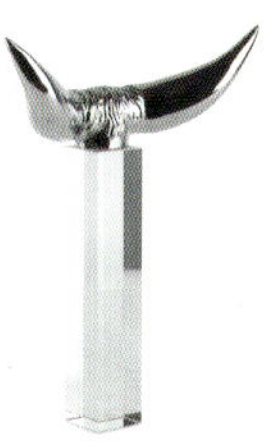

04 Abstract Decoration | 26cm×10cm×43cm

05 Chandelier | 50cm×50cm×97cm

06 Storage Box | 35cm×35cm×23cm

07 Clock | 22cm×22cm×22cm

08 Candlestick | 18cm×77cm

09 Photo Frame | 20.5cm×20.5cm×70.5cm

10 Human Form Decoration | 43cm×15cm×25cm

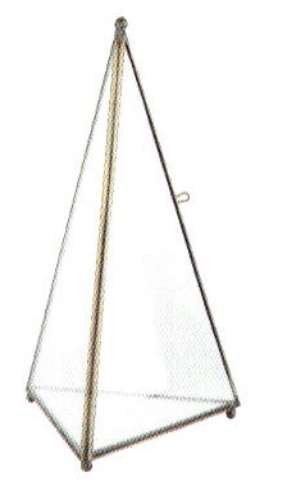

11 Abstract Decoration | 22cm×22cm×40cm

12 Candlestick | 22cm×11cm×41cm

13 Photo Frame | 21cm×2cm×26cm

14 Tray | 40cm×25cm×6cm

15 Double Sofa | 180cm×85cm×72cm

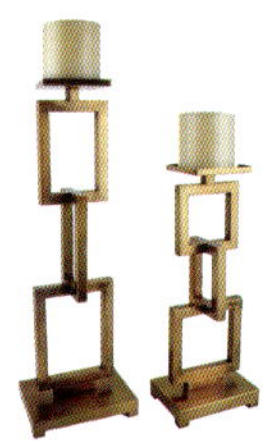

16 Mingshi — Candlestick | 20cm×16cm×61cm

18 Table Lamp

Size I 43cm × 76cm
Material I Iron & Fabric & Glass
Color I Transparent & Gold
Inspiration I Combination of Art Deco and Modern Home Furnishing
Style I Modern, American Style

17 Human Form Decoration

Size I 13cm × 6cm × 32cm
Material I Marble & Metallic
Color I Gold
Inspiration I Combination of Art Deco and Modern Home Furnishing
Style I Modern, Chinese Style, American Style

19 Candlestick

Size I 8cm × 9cm / 8cm × 4cm
Material I Iron & Oak Walnut
Color I Black
Inspiration I Combination of Art Deco and Modern Home Furnishing
Style I Modern, American Style

20 Bookend

Size I 15cm × 7cm × 21cm × 2PCS
Material I Marble & Metal
Color I White & Gold
Inspiration I Combination of Art Deco and Modern Home Furnishing
Style I Modern, American Style

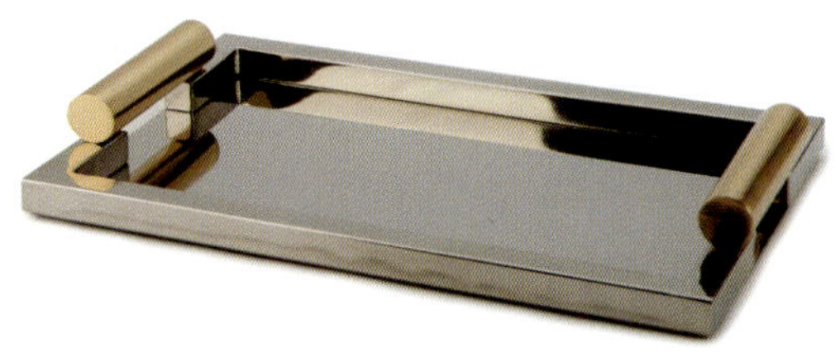

21 Tray

Size I 40cm × 25cm × 5cm
Material I Copper & Stainless Steel
Colors I Gold & Silver
Inspiration I Combination of Art Deco and Modern Home Furnishing
Style I Modern, American Style

22 Flower Container & Candlestick

Size I 15cm × 25cm
Material I Marble & Metal
Color I Transparent & Gold
Inspiration I Combination of Art Deco and Modern Home Furnishing
Style I Modern, American Style

24 Candlestick

Size I 120cm × 5cm × 37cm
Material I Iron
Color I Gold / Black
Inspiration I Combination of Art Deco and Modern Home Furnishing
Style I Modern, American Style

23 Snack Shelves

Size I 30cm × 15cm × 35cm
Material I Iron & Glass
Color I Gold
Inspiration I Combination of Art Deco and Modern Home Furnishing
Style I Modern

25 Magazine Rack

Size I 56cm × 15cm × 47cm
Material I Iron & Leather
Colors I Orange & Gold
Inspiration I Combination of Art Deco and Modern Home Furnishing
Style I Modern, Neo-Chinese Style

ORIENTAL NEW ARISTOCRACY

Elegant life

China is a poetic country, also an important source of oriental civilization.

From the tranquil leisure of "For I pick chrysanthemums under the eastern hedge, and far away to the south I can see the mountains," to the simple warmth of "There's a gleam of green in an old bottle. There's a stir of red in the quiet stove," from the romantic elegance of "Poetry and self-entertainment, fish are kept for viewing, cook tea and play with crane," to the peace of mind of "Detached view of the secular world, calm and comfortable in mind", ancient literati outline a quiet indifferent and harmonious cozy paradise for us.

With the evolution of history, now we have entered a highly developed industrial and commercial society. In a generally more impulsive era, people are always walking anxiously. In the modern bustling city filled with reinforced concrete, more people want to slow down to have an artistic and poetic life. "Look at the three thousand years of history, all people seek for whether fame, or wealth. But when you see through life, the ultimate quest is only plain life."

In the new era, the intellectuals are mostly highly educated, with a profound cultural background and knowledge connotation. They are playing an important role in various fields of society, with the elegant name "modern Oriental noble". These people pursue the sentiment, and their demand for life is beyond the material itself. They also want to enjoy themselves spiritually, so they desire an elegant and lively living place, surrounded by the cultural atmosphere. The intellectuals put more emphasis on the comfort and functionality, but not magnificent in deliberate. This tendency turns out that the Neo-Chinese life style is accepted by its gentle and elegant sentiment nowadays when the minimalism is popular. The honorable culture and the peaceful life style gradually return to our society, representing the recall for the rural China times. It is also a spiritual yearning of the idyllic life as well as the grand respect for the tranquil soul.

Elegant life, the pursuit of a refined attitude to life, is a blend of ancient and modern neo-classical way of life. It is from small to understand big things, and it cares more about consciousness than ceremony and more spirit than material. The Chinese elegant life will be out of the question without deep culture heritage and profound ideological content. With small bridge and water, pleasant music, listening to Kunqu Opera in front of the pavilion, travel the Taihu Lake in the snow with friends, together with a cup of tea, a pool of lotus, elegant life is so simple and easy to get. When autumn leaves fall in the rain, playing chess game, or the zither, or drawing, to find a relaxing place for the body in the elegant coziness, in fact, is a perfect choice for healthy temperament.

Zhou Zuoren also said: "We look at the sunset, watching the autumn river and the flowers, listening to the rain, smelling and drinking wine not to quench thirst, eating the snacks, though useless decorate, but the more refined the better." This is Chinese-style elegant life.

Elegant and unique,
beautiful and
unconventional

IMAGE © EASE WORKSHOP

IMAGE © EASE WORKSHOP

Chinese-style Elegant Charm

The Neo-Chinese Style is born in China's traditional culture revival period, accompanied by enhanced national strength and national consciousness. In the exploration of Chinese design community at the beginning of the local consciousness, mature new generation of design teams and consumer market nurture subtle beautiful Neo-Chinese Style. In the era of Chinese culture sweeping the world, soft Chinese elements and modern materials, the Ming and Qing Dynasties furniture, window lattices, fabric bed products bring out the best in each other, reproducing the scene of the exquisite pieces.

Concise aesthetic of classical Chinese charm, graceful character for thousands of years, transforms into a new look. The introverted and calm ancient China as the source, integrate into elements of fashion and pragmatism expression techniques. Ancient and modern, this infusion between Eastern and Western cultures, would definitely generate something incredible as a result, which also adds a distinctive elegance to the renovated Chinese-style, while maintaining the calmness from the traditional Chinese heritage.

Performance Techniques

The Neo-Chinese style pays attention to regularity and symmetry, balancing the concept of yin-yang to reconcile the indoor ecology. The use of natural decorative materials and "gold, wood, water, fire, soil," such combination of Five Elements creates a Zen-style rational and tranquil environment.

The space is often decorated with concise and clean straight lines, sometimes with panel-type furniture influenced by Western industrial design. Linear decoration in the use of space, not only reflects the pursuit of modern simple living requirements, but also does it meet the requirement of the Chinese furniture to pursue introverted, simple design style.

Decorative Space

The Neo-decoration is very particular about creating special levels. According to the capacity and privacy requirement, different functional spaces are often divided by cased openings or antique curio shelves; to keep certain space out of sight, screens and lattice window are often applied. With those approaches, unit-style residential house shows the beauty of Chinese-style home, especially in the smaller housing, which often results in "walk in scene" decorative effect. In the decorative details of respect for natural appeal, flowers, birds, fish and others, uncompromising attention to detail, full of change, all of which fully embodies the spirit of traditional Chinese aesthetics.

Modeling

Decorative space uses more concise and tough straight lines. The use of linear decoration in space, not only reflects the pursuit of modern simple living requirements, but also does it meet the requirement of the Chinese furniture to pursue introverted, simple design style, which makes the Neo-Chinese style more practical and modern.

Color

The Neo-Chinese style furniture is mostly dark-based color, matching with the wall color: firstly, the tone is based in black, white, gray of Suzhou gardens and Beijing houses; secondly, on the basis of the black, white and gray colors, red, yellow, blue, green colors and so on of the royal residence are as a local color.

Furniture

The Neo-Chinese style could be classical furniture only, or the combination of modern and classical furniture. The Ming and Qing Dynasty furniture is the representative of the Chinese classical furniture. In the Neo-Chinese style furniture, accessories take the concise-line style of Ming Dynasty style furniture as the principal thing.

Decorative Element

Silk, Yarn, Fabric, Cloth, Wallpapers, Glass, Antique Tiles, Marble, Calligraphy and Painting, Plaque, Hanging Screen, Chinaware, Antique, Earthenware, Screen, Personal Galleries, Round-backed Armchair, Carved Wood Window, Bonsai, Hydroponics, as well as a certain meaning of Chinese classical items, exquisite porcelain, meaningful decorative painting, perfectly introduce the passion collision of history and modern, classic and fashion.

4

EASE WORKSHOP

IMAGE © EASE WORKSHOP

IMAGE © EASE WORKSHOP

Weather changing with time, natural energy floating through the land, the beauty of the material, superb craftsmanship, only when the four of them are considered together, something great can be created.

4.1 LIVING ROOM

In the Chinese-style interior design, we should pay attention to light and dark colors arrangement. Placing some light-colored decorations in the dark furniture is a good match.

IMAGE © EASE WORKSHOP

In the living room, lines of wooden sofa are simple, and there is sense of texture rather cumbersome. The use of light-colored pillow and cushion with dark wood sofa, is neutralizing the serious sense.

IMAGE © EASE WORKSHOP

The moderate-sized ornaments in the center become a visual focus. Two book shelves are in symmetrical distribution, giving stability to the layout.

IMAGE © EASE WORKSHOP

Hangzhou Wangxing Ji Fan Exhibition Hall

In the more open space, you can use the plain beige or white walls decorated with a large traditional Chinese painting works, but its color must be coordinated to other furniture.

Chinese interior design style is usually calm. So in the living room and other space, you can use a number of pillows with lively colors and rich patterns to heighten the atmosphere.

IMAGE © EASE WORKSHOP

IMAGE © EASE WORKSHOP

In the linear Treasure Pavilion with rounded but curve vases and other ornaments, you can break a sense of seriousness brought by the straight line.

4.2 STUDY ROOM

IMAGE © EASE WORKSHOP

The traditional tough-lined wooden furniture with light-colored wall is a common mix of Chinese-style home furnishing.

Chinese style furniture with the full realization of ancient charm, has brought a very serious, elegant feeling. The whole setting allows that we can be truly exposed to the mood of ancient literati and fully aware of the majestic traditional culture.

4.3 BEDROOM

The use of the same series of Neo-Chinese style furniture helps the archaistic home furnishing blend in with modern elements, which avoids producing a very strong sense of ancient elegance but full of modern Chinese fashion personality style.

IMAGE © EASE WORKSHOP

White space is an important element in Chinese painting. It also plays a key role in Chinese design. The clean walls, dark furniture and floors create a low-key and quiet atmosphere. Wall is not linked to decoration, but bright and low-key.

4.4 PRODUCT DISPLAY

01 Refreshing Breeze | Leisure Chair

Size l 650mm×560mm×860mm
Comfortable breeze, and ethereal quiet. "Emptiness" means inclusiveness and greater possibilities. Works with clear water-like acrylic material show the concept of "emptiness", enabling the chair maintain this calm sprit under different circumstances.

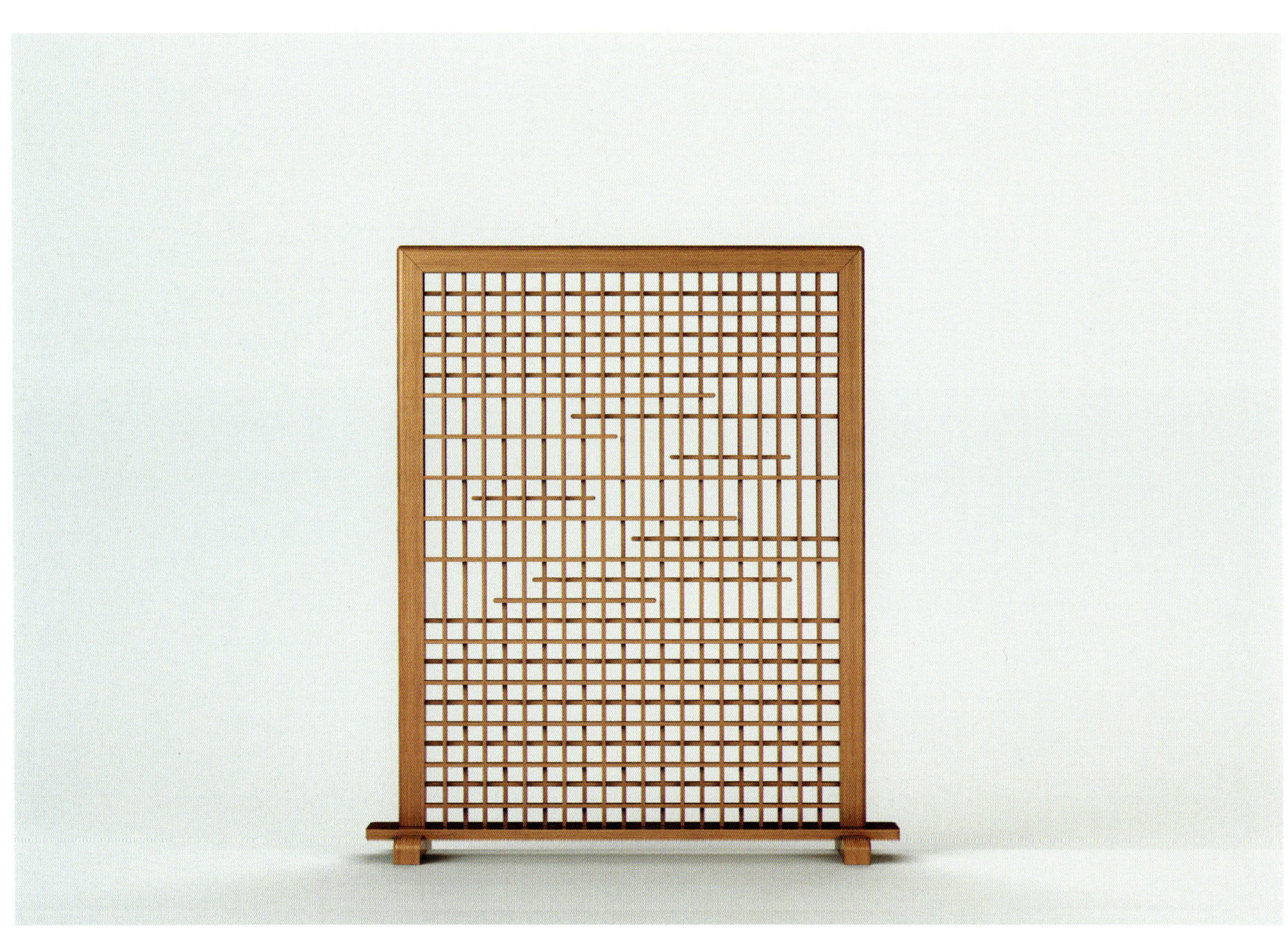

02 Suhuai Sparkling | Screen

Size l 1510mm × 380mm × 1665mm
In the landscape of lakes and hills, breeze is coming, and water is sparkling. It is inspired by the sparkling water surface. It transfers water reflection of landscape onto a vertical level, taking lines as the framework, and through the double-layer structure, parts of which reaching out for each layer to mimic the interaction between light and shadow, a modern and creative approach.

IMAGE © EASE WORKSHOP

03 Suhuai | Free Tune

Size | 680mm×593mm×815mm

Blowing the seven-string instrument, letting the music echo with running spring. Utilizing wood, cloth and acrylic as materials, the Free Tune expresses the flexibility and inclusiveness of liquid sprit and also the material colors transcend a gentle feeling.

04 Suhuai Slow Life | Zen Chair

Size | 950mm×830mm×620mm

The so-called Zen, assembles breeze and diffuses fragrance.

Designers believe that the pace of modern life is compact, which is so in need of silence and introspection time. It will re-design Zen chair to break its inherent image, and change its form and proportion to better integrate into the modern home furnishing life.

IMAGE © EASE WORKSHOP

05 Gold and Jade · Bright | Garden Stool

Size | 44mm×380mm×470mm
Shadow changes from time to time.
Appearance is sourced from the Chinese classical furniture. Garden stool frame is cut by laser, and lighting could be installed inside. "Leaves and flowers" mapped to the entire space creating a romantic art for life.

06 Gold and Jade · Frame | Leisure Chairs

Size I 630mm×590mm×840mm
It joins curved and straight, virtual and real, dynamic and static elements together.
The chair is designed to explore the collision between modern metal and oriental aesthetics. Through the forging process, the combination of curved and straight lines, the contrast of the thickness and the leather material, the chair presents a modern oriental charm.

5

CHUN ZAI DONG FANG

5.1 LIVING ROOM

IMAGE © CZDF

IMAGE © CZDF

The living room uses silk wallpaper of gold foil paint. Silk is an ideal material for interior furnishing given its soft touch and the slightly shiny pearl white surface. The room's colour scheme involves black, gold and apricot, the combination of which feels gentle and elegant, and this, together with the carefully crated furniture, create a sense of modern luxury but in a accessible way.

The space is inspired by the shapes and mountain and louts. The guests will first be greeted by light blue coloured lotus lamp and oil painting of continuous mountains, beyond them the cerulean blue background colour-matching with the carpet of water-coloured louts, giving the space a unique world view described in Chinese landscape poetry.

IMAGE © CZDF

Before the Western Han Dynasty (206BC-9AD), the Eastern and Western cultures had collided and merged through the Silk Roads. After the Emperor Wu of Han Dynasty, the Silk Roads in the Sea deepened the integration of Eastern and Western cultures. In fact, the mutual absorption of Eastern and Western cultures far exceeded our imagination. East and West culture in the development of the entire era of the timeline is on the inclusiveness. Elegant Oriental style and modern Western fashion flourish in our living life. Especially in today's blending of traditional culture and foreign aesthetic, CZDF brand's "East Love West Rhyme" is a Neo-Chinese style way of life under the westward spread of Eastern culture.

IMAGE © CZDF

IMAGE © CZDF

The ecological space with natural simplicity is achieved through the mottled wall and the Chinese style furniture.

"No Boundaries" focuses on users. It perceives senses and intends to create a large home furnishing lifestyle brand covering the color tone of the whole latitude.

Ancient Chinese ink painting is circulated in the world, and indifferent tone rings through thousands of years. The Chinese literati with their delicate pen draw "Sparse shadows reflect horizontally in the clear and shallow water, and scented fragrance floats around under the dusk moon". Lotus and moonlight never had any noise. Put into few slice of tea, raise tea cup, slowly pour into the boiling water.

IMAGE © CZDF

IMAGE © CZDF

5.2 HALLWAY DISPLAY

IMAGE © CZDF

5.3 PRODUCT DISPLAY

IMAGE © CZDF

01 XP17014 Leisure chair
Size l 60cm×64.5cm×76cm
Material l Lether / Zelkova

02 Six pottery figures of musician
Size l 10cm×8cm×16cm
Material l Ceramic / Wooden base

03 Table with pointed legs and nipple-pattered jade top
Size l 50cm×50cm×44cm
Material l Metal / Jade / Bronze legs

04 Rectangular box wiped in copper sheets, with stand
Size l 82cm×62cm×48cm
Material l Copper sheet / wood

05 XP17039 Closet

Size I 120cm × 40cm × 170cm
Material I Matte Jacobean wood stain /
Closet door upholstery

06 Over the boundary-PH980-5B

Size I 71cm × 18cm × 40cm
Material I Blank sand paint / Bronze / Matte white

07 Paired lying Lion figures

Size I 50cm × 50cm × 150cm
Material I Ceramic / Pseudo-classical process

08 Round table made of copper sheets (L / S)

Size I 90cm × 90cm × 35cm
60cm × 60cm × 43cm
Material I Oriented Strand Board /
Copper sheet / iron-made legs

09 Story of Empty-city Stratagem painted in contract colours, Kintsugi blue-and-white porcelain plate, JZJS007 (wooden stand included)

Size I H:44cm D:44cm
Material I Porcelain / Kintsugi

10 Bamboo and Cicadidae Serious PH309-13A

Size I 61cm × 15cm × 65cm
Material I Blank / Bronze, Volakas base

11 Kintsugi blue-and-white porcelain gourd-shaped Vessel painted with green birds in bamboo forest JZJS009

Size I H:33cm D:23cm W:23cm
Material I Porcelain / Kintsugi

12 Taihu Scholar Rock-PH841-1B

Size I 47cm × 17cm × 47.5cm
Material I Brushed titanium / Emerald green / Marble base

IMAGE © CZDF

VISUAL ART

VISUAL ART

"Autumn wind is bleak, and life has come to the period when maple leaves begin to turn red. The rest of the seasons is only winter. However, life is just a cycle of four seasons. After winter, life is over. No matter how much storage, it is useless. When young, everyone should be hard. But no matter what the results are, people are old, and have the right to rest and to enjoy time with their grandchildren around the knee. Autumn beauty of life, should not be sad to remember, not with the unwillingness to continue to struggle, but to enjoy thoroughly."

Yutang Lin "The Art of Life

The Art of Life

In his book "Art of Living," Mr. Lin tells us that, how to improve the quality of life apart from our work and responsibilities, to have a great taste of life, which is to enjoy life. People walking in a hurry and shuttling in the streets, are exhausted with life. In the eyes of many people, life gradually becomes a result or a goal. However, life should be enjoyed in peace and at ease.

Life is in thousands of postures. Will apperceptions of a sensitive heart be different from ordinary people? When thinking about how to make life not be a burden and not become the roller grinding our talent, but stimulate our creativity and beauty. Only to maximize the adaptation of nature can it achieve the spirit of freedom and liberation. Know the whole world from a small flower. In our daily life there are a lot of subtleties and unspeakable things, such as season, tide, impermanence of things, and so on. The unexpected experience is so fun from the nature. Life is art, and art also is life. Advocate the art of life, but also pursue artistic life. Since in ordinary life art is everywhere.

"Everyone is an artist" — German artist Joseph Beuys once said. Art is from life and higher than life. Art is from us both far and close, for that poetry and painting is art, tea is art, and in fact life is also an art. Life is mixed feeling and reflected in the daily trivia such as eating, walking, working, and studying. Comprehending art in life will make daily trivia no longer monotonous.

The purest beauty is from the nature. What we pursue in fact has been in the natural good fortune and quietly blooming. This stems from the attitude of life, so that art is as natural as breathing. The endless inspiration and encouragement make resource from trees that reflect the color of quiet blue sky, or a posture of blooming flowers in the spring which change and record our rich inspiration. We will consider a corner in the nature as a place for meditation and self-cultivation, to explore hidden taste between life and art in the balance.

Record the artistic way of life

IMAGE © BOKING ART

IMAGE © BOKING ART

Visual Art Gesture

From the beginning of human culture to today, human convey information through the visual image created by their own. Visual communication has always been the basic means of communication between people. These visual images are what we call "visual art" today. That is, with some materials, shaping visual art image of the plastic arts can be viewed by people. Modeling technique varied and the art image forms include sculpture, architectural art, decorative art and crafts and so on. Among them, the basic elements include: lines, shapes, light and dark, color, texture, space. These form the basis of a work. Design principles include: layout, contrast, rhythm, balance, unity. They are the principles and methods used by artists to organize and use basic elements to communicate meaning. Sculpture art is a kind of plastic arts, but also the manifestation of magic art form, also known as sculpture, sculpture and shaping in general. To create a visual and palatable artistic image with a certain space, in order to reflect the social life, to express the artist's aesthetic feeling, aesthetic emotion and aesthetic ideal, with the help of plastic (such as gypsum, resin, clay, etc.) or carving (such as metal, wood, stone, etc.).

There are thousands of objects in the world, which are diverse in content selection. Ranging from cosmic astrology to proton structure, from conscious subject reproduction to randomness composition, as long as there is a meaningful form, it can be expressed in the sculpture. Beautiful and mysterious crystal glass art work is very simple and pure in shape. If you want to create a unique color and lighting effects, you need to go through a series of complex processes. Cutting, laminating, carving and refining solid-state glass is critical for each step. Creating a variety of internal geometries patterns depends on how the array is arranged. It produces semi-permeable, frosted, faded halo and other more advanced texture after exposure to light, as if a processing of light to absorb the magic stone, and the light is locked in them. Appearance of the concise and complex internal contradictions constitutes a distinct body. The glass also has transparent and translucent properties, the perfect metaphor of the complexity and contradictions of life, making people read the aftertaste for a long time, with impulse to touch and play.

When growing-disappeared hand-made comes back to the contemporary society where everyone's eyes are focused on form and idea over all the things, the sculpture is not only a return to manual labor, but also deepest feelings of the most sincere arousal of human heart. These crystal glass works contain much principle of form beauty and enduringly form an irresistible "beauty" force. Its shape comes from accumulation of daily life, and the performance reflects a strong interest of life. It is filled with a particular era of secular life to embody personalized image. The way is rough yet concise, and fully demonstrates the beauty of nature and harmony.

6

BOKING ART OF GREAT PURITY

IMAGE © BOKING ART

The highest excellence in the like that of water.

"The best of man is like water, which benefits all things, but strives for nothing."
In the Tao Te Ching of Laozi.

4500mm × 1300mm × 1000mm

As Good As Water

When BOKING ART met craftsmen, You will see it blooming out of another style.

Flexible degree, simplified appropriately, bending and straightening suitably, combining force with mercy, which is also full of music rhythm.

Laozi said: "Tao that can be described is not universal and eternal Tao. Name that can be named is not universal and eternal Name." We can understand that the Tao is natural and unspeakable. Laozi advocated the harmony of nature with "Great music has the faintest notes, great form is beyond shape", and was extended by the artists of the BOKING ART as advocating naturalism without leaving too many artificial carvings. It is just the beauty to the point.

Three-Dimensional Ink & Wash

Breeze, Moon, Cloud and Zen

195mm×195mm×510mm

195mm×195mm×570mm

195mm×195mm×565mm

195mm×195mm×510mm

IMAGE © BOKING ART

300mm×300mm×400mm

The log and deadwood with technology approach is sealed permanently in the platinum crystal, then after careful hand-polishing, it turns into unique stool. Surprises are here.

510mm×470mm×660mm

The soothing water flow gives a sense of inward condensation. Between ideological and practical the visual center is exceptionally vivid.

360mm×360mm×600mm

Φ1100mm

IMAGE © BOKING ART

Low-back Chair

Wood · Luxury

Using high-tech transparent material moulding process artists present the "new luxury" doctrine. Each work is unique, made of rotten wood, dead branches, leaves that after years of baptism already left with time traces. Artists use artisan spirit to create a series of works of art, so dead wood, dead branches and leaves breathe, glowing new lives. Time seems to be still, but life has been sublimated.

IMAGE © BOKING ART

3200mm×500mm×800mm

Boking Taihu Stone

600mm×550mm×1700mm

IMAGE © BOKING ART

She looked around, static yet dynamic. It is so lifelike that we almost hear breathing.

Carving in unique perspective rules,

pay attention to metaphysical freehand spirit. Without too formal decoration.

She only has the real expression, lyrical body language, conveying to us indifferent life posture.

270mm×320mm×980mm

500mm×550mm×1700mm

520mm×220mm×820mm

Vast Landscape

Dialogue between contemporary and ancient people across time and space, pursuit of Tao & Qi in Chinese classical landscape through artistic language.

800mm×600mm×5000mm

CLASSICAL ARISTOCRACY

Quality Life

In 2010, "Downton Abbey" was broadcasted in ITV. Subsequently, the drama about the life of the British noble, appeared in the Emmy and Golden Globe Awards and other list of winners. The drama's success depends on, in addition to exciting story, vivid Aristocratic life, overflowing aristocratic spirit and classical elegance of the interior decoration which is the absolute highlight.

Pay attention to the aristocratic style, in particular value the style and quality of life. Everyone may look forward to the elegant noble life, wearing high-level customization of the elegant dress, elegantly bringing up a glass of red wine or champagne to attend a variety of social Cocktail party, or dressed in extreme-perfection handsome riding habit in leisure hunting time or enjoying the afternoon tea with British rituals in the elegantly furnished residence. The greatest charm of noble life is not extravagance, nor a big house or the number of servants, but it is the spirit revealed from the bones, the details of life, that indeliberately and naturally showing the noble aristocratic temperament.

In "Downton Abbey" the scene that manservant irons newspaper for earl impresses audience so deeply for the exquisite life. Such small thing is so delicate, let alone its daily residential decoration.

Fashion is a trend, and aristocracy is a kind of accumulation

IMAGE © DI GAO MEI JU

European and American classical style

European classical decoration style

European classical charm lies in its unique historical traces which reflect the elegant timeless bearing on behalf of an excellent quality of life of owner.

European classical style is evolved from the aristocratic lifestyle, which contains elements just to meet the demand for lifestyle of current cultural bourgeois, namely: a sense of culture, a sense of nobility, no lack of a sense of freedom and mood, but also the pursuit of history and culture, which is not only reflected in the ornaments on the antique works of art, but also reflected in the decoration of various antique tiles, stone preferences and the pursuit of a variety of antique processes. In general, the classical aristocratic style of decoration is elegant and full of history.

European classical style with gorgeous decoration, strong colors, beautiful shape to achieve the elegant decoration effect, vividly embodies the rich cultural heritage of European culture. The style presentation is extremely particular, giving the impression of dignified and elegant, noble and gorgeous, with a strong cultural atmosphere. Furniture matching generally uses large fine furniture, together with the exquisite carving. The overall effects create a gorgeous, noble, warm feeling. It often uses golden and brown accessories to bring out the noble and elegant classic of furniture. In color, it often uses white or yellow series as the basis, with dark green, dark brown, gold, etc., showing the classical European style luxury temperament. In material, it generally uses cherry wood, walnut and other high-end solid wood, showing noble and elegant aristocratic temperament.

American classical decoration style

American classical style is rooted in European culture, and it abandoned the Baroque and Rococo style which pursued novel and flashy, and was based on a new understanding of classic, emphasizing concision, clear lines and elegant, decent decoration.

American classical style formed a mixed one in the transmission of European culture and combined with the characteristics of their own culture of the United States.

Referring to elements and characteristics of classical and neo-classical style is a major bright spot of American classical style. Decoration material of American classical style is mainly hard and gorgeous. Bright color is less. Curtains and wallpaper also choose soft colors. To create a warm classical temperament, it abandons the magnificent European-style temperament to focus on practicality and coordination of the overall home furnishing.

American classical style decoration considers the various uses of each space. The American classical style living room is relatively low and gentle which selects comfortable and soft material and pays attention to family atmosphere. American classical style furnishings are also very distinctive. The main colors are black, dark red, brown and other dark colors. American classical style furniture prefers darker color that looks stable and elegant. The bed has a high column and veiling. The graceful bed mantle can present elegant beauty of the American classical style. Also, American classical style chair highlights the characteristics of the "Queen Anna", and American furniture carving through aging treatment, wormhole, erosion and other embellishments displays the beauty of American classic.

IMAGE © DI GAO MEI JU

Classic ornaments soft decoration matching skills

New classical furniture in recent years developed fast in domestic market showing a good momentum of development. Classical, neo–classical furniture of historical heritage, compared with modern plate–typed furniture, has a more profound cultural background. Therefore, the layout of classical home furnishings, including matching of furniture, lighting and ornaments, needs more ingenuity and more skills.

Choice of ornaments color

Furniture accessories are embellishment for the furniture, making furniture more luxurious and high-end, and to express foil effect of ornaments is the ability to control the performance of the entire space for designers. In the choice of ornaments the first is the same color matching, with the color to be similar or close, and furniture in harmony with the overall unity will produce the overall beauty.

Select ornaments similar to furniture

European, American classical furniture have their own unique technology and production processes. For each manufacturer the details of furniture such as hardware inlay and exquisite carving will be different, which inevitably requires furniture accessories in the style and appearance adapted to furniture. Similar carving patterns have a harmonious beauty. When European-style patterns match American-style furniture there will be the feeling of mistaken identity.

Distinguish the main color, sub-color and embellishment

Place ornaments in a bright layering. In an exhibition hall there should not be just one tone which is inevitably monotonous. There must be a sub-tone in addition to the main color, thus to form a sense of hierarchy. With the main, sub-tone color, ornament exhibition hall is not perfect but also needs different types or colors of ornaments which have played a focal point in the entire exhibition. It is just like that dropping a stone in calm water and ripples make water surface dynamic.

Allocation in line with the aesthetic

The entire home furnishings should be like a set of traditional Chinese painting. It is a sort of skill from composition to coloring. The rationality placement of furniture affects the level; color harmony affects the appearance. The perfect matching of furniture and accessories is embodiment of texture and nobility. Accessories are usually placed in two ways: from point to line and then to the surface, or vice versa, from the surface to the line and then to the point. Designers can choose the way to display.

Beauty lies in the details

Ornaments are placed in the general practicing of the "Round and square with the pursuit of harmonious development" theory. Take bedside cabinet as an example. After choosing the concordant style, color and ornaments, if surface is a square, the shape of furniture should be round or oval, vice versa. The match between ornaments is also important. Pay attention to the height of the accessories: if furniture is upright and foursquare, the accessories should be flexible, or follow low-high-low or high-middle-low. If furniture is round, ornaments should be structured. Height difference should not be too large.

7

DI GAO MEI JU

IMAGE © DI GAO MEI JU

CREATIVE walls
CICO BOOKS
THE SCARPETTA FACTOR
Patricia Cornwell

Every detail of exquisite hand-painted patterns is superb. Exquisite lacquering technology and high color saturation make the fresh green striking and pure, as if a heartbeat of love.

7.1 LIVING ROOM

IMAGE © DI GAO MEI JU

DC Outlets

IMAGE © DI GAO MEI JU

Love of copper objects can be described as a complex. Childhood in a sense should be called the copper years. No toys, but pick up coins, copper and others from beach. Hide them in the pocket in addition to a few pieces of copper shells. Love its high-quality texture and heavy sense of reality when you place it in the hands, with a proud attitude such as gold to highlight bright light, but with a humble low-key attitude to interpret the dignity and ancient rhyme.

IMAGE © DI GAO MEI JU

7.2 DINING ROOM

IMAGE © DI GAO MEI JU

IMAGE © DI GAO MEI JU

Craft production of the restaurant furniture is meticulous, in which there are hand-painted applications, gold and silver platinum features selections. All is beautiful. As long as you spend some extra patience and use those seemingly unimportant props with the suitable shape and color, you can easily create a romantic sweet lovers' world!

7.3 PRODUCT DISPLAY

IMAGE © DI GAO MEI JU

It uses a large number of complex carving processes, partly pasting gold foil. Some combinations are also with a small amount of black trim, and even more elegant. It symbolizes the international low-key luxury, filled with taste and fashion. Through the space furnishing display, it awakens people to deepen feelings to the art of home life, and enjoy the extraordinary luxury and royal life.

Ceramic inlay copper

Ceramic with copper is precision casting process which can create thin-walled and beautiful-outlined copper sculpture.

Derived from the exotic Spanish style, it uses fine grinding and polishing process to forge a smooth and sharp metal texture.

Design is sourced from abroad collection of antique masterpieces and copy hand-painted pattern. Organic combination of two different elements with a thick and sharp copper texture and simple natural ceramic overflow thick classical culture.

02 Size | 24.5cm × 18cm × 58.5cm

01 Size | 30.5cm × 22.5cm × 35.5cm

03 Size | 34cm × 34cm × 72.5cm

04 Size | 50cm × 20cm × 68.5cm

05 Size | 26cm × 26cm × 33.5cm

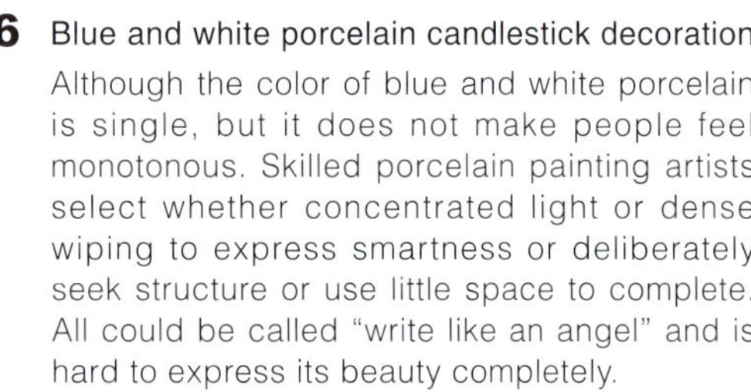

06 Blue and white porcelain candlestick decoration

Although the color of blue and white porcelain is single, but it does not make people feel monotonous. Skilled porcelain painting artists select whether concentrated light or dense wiping to express smartness or deliberately seek structure or use little space to complete. All could be called "write like an angel" and is hard to express its beauty completely.

07 Size | 25cm × 25cm × 63cm

08 Size | 23.5cm × 21cm × 45cm

09 Copper with ceramic porch

Copper sculpture with complex shape, fine pattern and multifarious process, highlights the extraordinary quality of the European palace furniture. In the entrance hall it manufactures magnificent concrete microcosm, giving a stunning sense.

10 Deer head wall clock

This is a "wall clock" of Rococo style, with a beautiful deer head and asymmetrical leaf decoration around the dial.

11 "Gigant" clock

"Gigant" clock is a very beautiful Louis XVI style table clock. The model is casted in the shape of building, and there are a lot of branch decoration on the front and side.

IMAGE © DI GAO MEI JU

Retro and classic merged into the superb skills

01 Hand-painting

Hand-painting process is complex. Brushing several times, elution and a specific halo technology in the production process can make the color of home accessories better integrated, and increase the rich layering for the pattern. Also, its use is very flexible, matching the temperament of the corresponding pattern according to the different styles of furniture, but also can choose brushwork, watercolor, oil painting and other options in the style of painting. The series of home accessories are decorated with exquisite hand-painting for the surface of the plain wood and ceramic home accessories to put on elegant clothes and add a rich sense of emotional elements and aesthetic appeal.

02 Ceramics

China is one of the earliest countries to apply pottery in the world, and Chinese porcelain has been highly respected by the world because of its high practicality and artistic quality. The series of ceramic products are concise and generous without losing elegance. Its shape, glaze and decoration have created an implication of art image.

03 Pourie inlay technology

Famous master of the palace furniture of France, Pourie develops creatively exquisite inlay wood craft in which the metal plate and the tortoise shells overlap to cut into patterns and are embedded in the furniture surface, forming a Pourie aristocratic decoration style and becoming main style of the French Rococo period. Unfortunately, the process has defect that "patch may fall off with the passing of time".

The series of home accessories inherit precious craftsmanship, while improving it to a higher level. These products use hand-painting simulation process to restore the precious wood chip mosaic collage effect, and the original metal shell mosaic is updated to gold foil mosaic. It not only retains the beauty of the mosaic process, but also is easy for collection and maintenance and enhances the overall furniture value.

05 Blue and white porcelain

Blue and white porcelain as a representative of the history of Chinese ceramics, is a symbol of ancient Chinese cultural heritage. It acculturates profound Chinese culture into the West, and has an indelible role in the process of cultural exchanges between China and foreign countries. Blue and white colors in opposite, simple and bright, hearty and generous, is the beauty of elegant fresh. Blue and white record the classic tastes, and delicate lines with elegant structure construct classical artistic concept.

04 Antique technology

Painting antique aging treatment is an important process of antique furniture, which uses a series of techniques for the new furniture to increase the ancient sense and to give a long history of imprinting. When restoring historical style it also adds unique human value to furniture. As "classic from the museum", "DI GAO MEI JU" home accessories use extensively painting antique craft to restore pieces of classical paintings and classic ornaments in museums in real arena, and this process is also perfectly shown in single item.

06 Gilding techniques

Inlay gold (or silver) is an ancient traditional craft. European palace home accessories are mostly gold foil surface, once exclusive for royal family and the nobility, a symbol of status and wealth. "DI GAO MEI JU" has inherited and improved gilding techniques on the basis of traditional process. The surface sprayed primer paint of the furniture has been sprayed a special background color in hand brush or spray, with a viscous water aqua in the background on the special treatment, and attached to the gold foil, creating a variety of artistic effects in close to the furniture accessories of the gold foil surface. Gilding technology allows the furniture accessories to maintain the luxury of the European-style palace expression. Gold foil and the surface of the furniture accessories are closely connected, illustrating the exquisiteness and luxury.

07 Dewax casting process

To highlight the extraordinary quality of European-style palace furniture and to restore the real material of palace furniture, the luxury series of ceramic ornaments use mostly copper castings decorative style. Copper decorations often use dewax casting process. Cere method is a precision casting process which can create copper sculpture with thin-walled, complex shape, fine pattern, and complex process.

In the making process, casting process is used to make the paraffin wax model. The sculptured shell is made of quartz sand and other casting material. Then, the shell is dewaxed and baked again, and then the copper water is poured. Broken shell after copper water is cooling to complete copper products. Finally, the surface of copper is to deal with coloring, corrosion and other treatment, so as to complete the sculpture production. It decorates ceramic surface with exquisite bronze, highlighting the extraordinary identity and style of furniture immediately.

NATURAL COMFORT

Return to rural home

Suddenly we start to be tired of the city. We are not accustomed to the hustle and bustle, the calculation between people, especially the more disturbing air, water and food, making it more powerless. We don't want to change the world, and there is no such ability. But we can change ourselves and our way of life. If everyone in the city chooses a wish, perhaps half of the people want to have a house in the city where they live, and the other half might hope to leave the city one day. Where shall we go when leave the city? Of course we will go to more suitable rural areas and have a rural life.

"Two acres of dry farmland, one clay-tiled home, a cow, a dog, a cat, a pair of chickens; sunset time to rest, dig wells to drink water, farming for food, live a happy life." From the beginning of the development of industrial society, there has been a reflection of urban civilization to return to the pastoral, and now it is more popular. However, world is changing and the most traditional pattern of farmers' life is hard to find. There are little mood of real farmers among urban people: "simple heart with no pursuit of luxury and greed. Live a life without restlessness, physically tired but spiritually relaxed."

The prosperity of city is not the forefront of trend of life, but the return to the traditional pastoral life is the ideal pursuit. Many people have begun to make the original desire for pastoral life gradually become a reality. This is the purpose of the chapter: behind the idyllic dream, a new way of life rises. Now the process of urbanization is getting faster and faster, while the traditional poetic villages inadvertently decline. However, people's inner garden dream is more and more intense. Step on the soil, pull a few radishes, pick a few tomatoes, rub directly by hands, bite one, mouthful of natural fragrance... simple and almost monotonous behavior allows people never bored for a long time in the city cages. Field ridges, vegetable garden, the sun and the fragrance of soil deliver the ideal pastoral world.

So, the way of life in the poem "We open your window over garden and field. Talk about mulberry and hemp with our cups in our hands", "While picking asters under the Eastern fence, my gaze is upon the Southern mountain rests" has been re-picked up and re-interpreted. People also hope that in their small home in the reinforced concrete forest they can still have their own pieces of "paradise." In the context, the most important thing is the contentment and calm state of mind and no disturbance by the material life, the unity of internal and external as well as the spirit and material. People are afraid to lose the existing items, in fact, more like a reaction to the fear of loss of social status. Changing the fundamental habits of life in fact demands one's starting to consider way of thinking. One who has too much material thing is a beggar. Richness is a state of mind rather than appearance. You may appreciate the beauty of the world that can be seen everywhere when you know how to appreciate the beauty of a flower.

Bustling faded, fresh leisure and back to nature.

FRENCH DRY
AGE © GLOBAL VIEWS

Pastoral leisure

Modern living room in the pastoral style design advocates "return to nature". Only by combining nature, can we obtain a balance between physical and psychological in today's fast-paced social life. So the pastoral style showing the natural pastoral life just meets the people's concern for rapid expansion, urban environment deterioration, increasing estrangement between people etc.

After a busy day outside, we really want to head into our own home, and thoroughly enjoy the comfort of the recliner and the warmth of sunshine through the windows, and enjoy the fragrance of wood furniture distribution, and even a fireplace in the winter while watching a wonderful novel. British countryside respected by Lin Yutang is certainly a representative of pastoral style. British pastoral style was formed around the end of the 17th century, mainly due to people's boredom of the luxury style, they are longing for the fresh rustic style.

Feature
Floral pattern is the eternal main theme of English pastoral style. Furniture is mostly hand-fabric-based cloth, with beautiful lines and elegant colors. Ornament cloth is also adhering to the distinctive feature making it unforgetable.

Cloth
Beautiful and handmade cloth has pretty color and takes numerous flowers as the main pattern. There are also floral, stripes, Scotland lattice, and every kind of cloth is full of local flavor.

Material
English pastoral furniture often uses pine and piles. Its production and carving are all handmade and very particular about color. Furniture is mostly white, ivory and other white-based, with elegant shape, detailed lines and high-grade paint treatment, making every product like a mature and elegant middle-aged woman exuding calmness and elegance, but also like a 18-year-old girl who has pure and refined temperament, arousing continuous imagination.

American village belonged to the natural style can also meet expectation of "home", which gives you happiness, as if walking through the golden wheat field on your way back home, humming leisurely. American country style is pleasant, elegant and leisure in appearance, which advocates "return to nature", and strives to show leisure, comfortable, natural pastoral life.

Feature
American country style emphasizes rural comfort design criteria to pursue the original material sense and pay attention to comparison between roughness of the material itself and fineness of workmanship.

Color
Take elegant slate and antique white as main tone, and free graffiti floral pattern for the mainstream characteristics. Line is in free style but clean and distinct. Delicate and uniform color, gorgeous and low-key pattern are full of rich flavor of life.

Material
It is usually with simplified lines, rough size. The selection is also very broad: solid wood, printed cloth, hand-woven nylon material, linen fabrics and natural cutting stone... It often uses natural wood, stone, rattan, bamboo, red brick and other materials without polish, to show rustic texture; take practical-oriented principal to commonly use pine, oak and others to decorate to show a sense of old.

8

FLOLENCO

IMAGE © FLOLENCO

Robison Crusoe
Robison Crusoe
Robison Crusoe
LES MISERABLES
Count of Monte Cristo

IMAGE © FLOLENCO

8.1 LIVING ROOM

8.2 DINING ROOM

8.3 PRODUCT DISPLAY

8.1 LIVING ROOM

Light blue fabric sofa matches the bright yellow leather sofa making the entire space light and stylish. Elm aging treatment bookcase without carving can still maintain the original texture and vein to bring more sense of layering for the whole space. Adding white elegant tea sets and marine style table lamp, we can experience complex romance and elegance, which embodies a beauty of style and expresses the comfortable beauty of life.

IMAGE © FLOLENCO
Horses

The series of living room has distinguished classic, calm temperament, and elegant colors, with both beautiful modeling and practical function. In the choice of material it is very critical. Solid wood of leather with the epidermis aging treatment exudes a low-key sense of luxury, reflecting the classical sense of elegance and utility of classical American style. In the use of color, with black, coffee and brown-based, the type of color in the home furnishing has good effects, dirtproof and easy to care. It is also elegant in the production of furniture. With high aesthetic and practical value, large furniture decorated with animal elements of the home accessories makes space more vivid.

IMAGE © FLOLENCO

LES MISERABLES
LES MISERABLES

IMAGE © FLOLENCO

This set of living room series is fashion and avant-garde, and its material and color are novel and bold. Black and white colorlessness embellishes bright orange to make the space more fresh and playful. Products abandon too many complicated decorations, and adopt natural concise lines to create a stylish and modern atmosphere. High contrast between high-reflective stainless steel and black & white stripes wallpaper complements each other, and vivid modeling ornaments make space more interesting.

The series of dining table is exquisite and fashionable with strong visual impact. It continues composition elements and spatial characteristics of the living room, with bright and bold colors as well as avant-garde and playful features. Coral shells on the table are filled with the breath of life. Wine-glasses chandeliers are full of creation and reflect the dazzling light in the light irradiation.

8.2 DINING ROOM

IMAGE © FLOLENCO

K
SUCCESS
IS THE
BEST
REVENGE

8.3 PRODUCT DISPLAY

IMAGE © FLOLENCO

01 Shiraz three-seat sofa

Size I 215cm×90cm×90cm
Material I Linen cloth

02 Taichi bookcase

Size I 112cm×42cm×220cm
Material I Oak, Stainless steel

03 Tree branches Candlestic

Size I 32cm×15cm×53cn
Material I Iron, Resin

04 Pinos Decorative Tank A / B

Size I 20cm×20cm×42cm / 28cm
Material I High Temperature Ceramics

IMAGE © FLOLENCO

05 Electronic Candle — Orange A / B

Size I 7.5cm × 12.5cm / 9cm
Material I Built-in 5 batterie

06 Black pallet

Size I 38cm × 48cm
Material I Wood, glass

07 Onyx Table Lamps — Red

Size I Lamp body 21cm × 10cm × 48cm
cover 35cm × 35cm × 26cm
Material I Agate tablets (Natural materials, agate shape of each product is different, and there are color differences)

08 Onyx Table Lamps — Blue

Size I Lamp body 21cm × 10cm × 48cm
cover 35cm × 35cm × 26cm
Material I Agate tablets (Natural materials, agate shape of each product is different, and there are color differences)

09 High-back chair — Red

Size I 42cm × 50cm × 107cm
Material I Oak, Thick fabric, Imitation leather

10 Peiqi convex mirror

Size I 52cm × 52cm × 8cm
Material I MDF, Convex mirror

11 Spar decorative painting D

Size I 40cm × 40cm × 5cm
Material I Solid wood frame, Natural ore

12 Ancient Greek lamp

Size I 85cm × 45cm
Material I Aluminum Plating Nickel

13 NISI Triple — Orange Materials

Size I 215cm × 90cm × 80cm
Material I Linen cloth

14 Ike cans — red AB

Size I 15.5cm × 15.5cm × 48cm/
14.5cm × 14.5cm × 42cm
Material I High temperature ceramics

15 Blue ripple lamp
Material I High temperature ceramics, transparent base

16 Shells and Western food sets
Material I Copper alloys

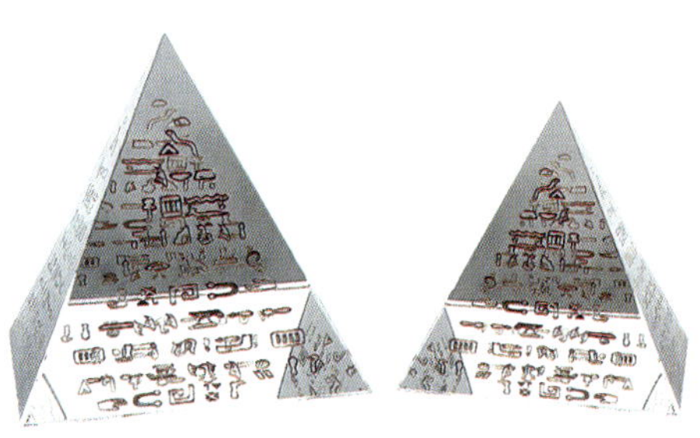

17 Crystal Pyramid AB
Size I 10cm×10cm×11cm/8cm×9cm
Material I K9 crystal material

18 XINUO tea sets
Material I Copper

19 Danny picture frame AB
Size I 15cm × 4.38cm × 20cm/12.5cm × 4.38cm × 15cm
Material I Aluminum plating copper

20 Paul barrels A
Size I 25cm × 15cm × 20cm
Material I Brass with nickel plating

IMAGE © FLOLENCO

21 Darth vases
Size I 25cm×39.5cm
Material I Copper Nickel Plated, Genuine leather

22 Orchid Decoration A
Size I 30cm×30cm×30cm
Material I Brass plate plated in light gold

23 Jamie decorative ball AB
Size I 13cm×17cm /10×14cm
Material I Cow bone, Brass base

24 Shells petals napkin clasp
Material I Shell handmade string

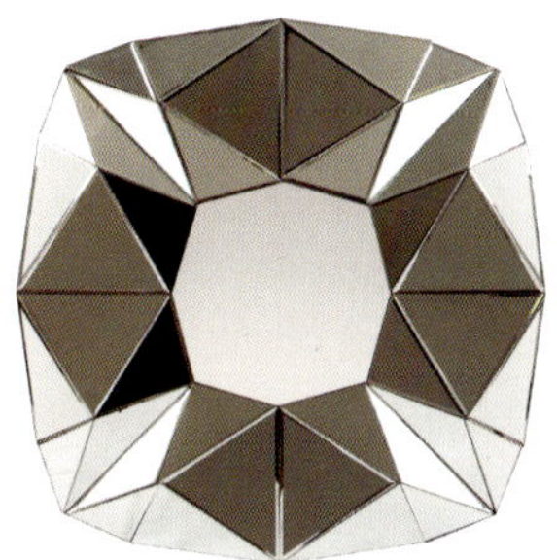

25 Mogh mirror
Size I 76.2cm×76.2cm×5.1cm
Material I MDF, Mirror

26 Clay tea table — silver
Size I 63.75cm×36.88cm×52.5cm
Material I Aluminum, Copper

27 LIKE entrance frame

Simple and neat materials like brass and glass, with square and concise profile shape and lines, modernization transformation of the classic shape, material, which is not exaggerated, but to create a subtle sense of fantasy, let everything orderly.

28 Leather baskets

As if transfigure the old cortex into practical container, emitting a distant sense of the era, enriching monotonous indoor, increasing the sense of accumulation of space, revealing the durability and perseverance of time.

29 England carpet

Scottish Check is the most representative check pattern of the British style. The classic check has been given modern interpretation by designer, with more complex lines and check as well as the hand-woven texture.

31 Scallop Decorations

Artificial alloy and natural shell in integration turn into unique creative handmade ornaments, just like back to the beach to listen to sea breeze blowing and the waves roaring...

30 Sini Box Coffee Tables

With aluminum skin, MDF fiberboard and simulation skin as the material, it becomes old box coffee tables for nostalgia people. Nostalgic elements create a thick old color, with a tough temperament to interpret the retro style of industry.

IMAGE © FLOLENCO
图片来自佛洛伦克品牌

32 Aspen table lamp — black
Size I 84cm × 50cm
Material I Copper Nickel Plated

33 Black and white striped chairs
Size I 49cm × 57cm × 94cm
Material I Beech

34 Checkered plate A/B
Size I 28cm × 28cm × 2.5cm/
19cm × 19cm × 2cm
Material I Bone china

35 Mis three-seat sofa

Size I 229cm×99cm×80cm
Material I Oil wax or Imitation leather

36 Fur photo frame

Import
Size I 19cm×25cm
Material I Hand rub color and aging treatment cattle leather

37 Sino decoration A/B/C

Import
Size I 15cm×15cm×50cm/13cm×13cm×42cm/11cm×11cm×35cm
Material I Aluminium, Cattle bone

38 Cattle leather round tray
Import
Size | 40cm × 40cm × 5cm
Material | Hand rub color and aging treatment cattle leather

40 The zebra pillow
Import
Size | 45cm × 45cm
Material | Wool, Cotton

39 Leopard Dog AB
Size | 24.5cm × 10cm × 22cm/13.5cm × 9cm × 20cm
Material | Resin Copper Plating

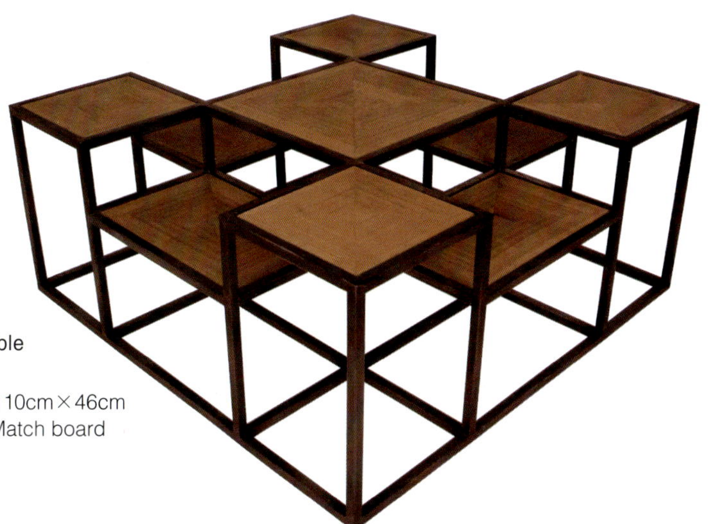

41 North coffee table
Import
Size | 110cm × 110cm × 46cm
Material | Iron, Match board

42 Lenny sofa
Size | 64cm × 70cm × 92cm
Material | Imitation leather or oil wax skin

43 Cox three-seat sofa
Size | 210cm × 88cm × 110cm
Material | Linen cloth

44 SINY Box coffee table
Size | 120cm × 70cm × 50cm
Material | Aluminum skin, MDF, Simulation leather

45 SINY six drawers cabinet
Size | 60cm × 50cm × 120cm
Material | Aluminum skin, MDF, Simulation leather

IMAGE © FLOLENCO

46 SIQI three-seat sofa
Size I 228cm×92cm×95cm
Material I Linen cloth

47 Crystal ball decoration A/C
Size I 26cm×35cm/18cm×27cm
Material I Glass

48 LIKE long coffee table
Size I 111cm×61cm×55cm
Material I Brass

BRAND SPONSORS

GLOBAL VIEWS

Global Views was founded in 1997 in Dallas, US. The main business is global high-end products and high-end space design and implementation. Brand founder David Gebhart spent 15 years on in-depth understanding of product design and customer preference, paving the way for Global Views' many years of retail procurement experience, strong product development capabilities, and professional marketing knowledge from the very beginning of the establishment.

OMENIA

"Stainless steel household goods experts" is the core concept of Omenia brand. Omenia advocates minimalism and modern art, and the main material of products is stainless steel, using extensive of environmentally friendly metal materials. The products include creative furniture, art decoration, tea sets, kitchen supplies, and hotel supplies and so on.

WELAND

Guangzhou Weland Handicraft Co., Ltd. was founded in 2007, with brands AMES, Luxor and EXP +. Based on the Pearl River Delta, Weland is characterized by the integration of handicraft sales and space hard and soft decoration program. Different from the strong visual design of modern home furniture, Weland advocats lifestyle focusing on user experience and creating a living atmosphere. Weland is committed to making living space conducive to people's daily communication and emotional sublimation. It is to restore life and beautify life, rather than a fine but not practical, nice but not warm house.

EASE WORKSHOP

Ease workshop was founded in 2011. Following the idea of "the example of nature as a teacher, free symbiotic", and through the combination of traditional and modern technology, as well as the use of diversified materials, it adapts to the contemporary life of people, objects, space relations, so to achieve symbiosis between people and society, people and nature. In retrospect to Oriental Zen aesthetic and integration of modern Western design concepts, it is committed to creating the modern Oriental home brand blending natural, humanities, design in one. It has won several awards at home and abroad.

CHUN ZAI DONG FANG

CZDF incorporates research and development, production, sales and soft decoration design in one, to provide customers with "Neo-Chinese style" cultural home accessories one-stop overall soft decoration services. With the keen sense of Chinese culture and home furnishing trends, CZDF forms an "international, fashional, Oriental" research and development team, and takes the lead in proposing the "Neo-Chinese style" concept of the overall home furnishing. Products cover ceramics, lighting, decorative painting, wood, screens, furniture, sculpture, wallpaper and other home furnishing accessories.

Its household products have five major brand series and two design agencies. The brand "Hua Tian Imagination" focuses on the design of Neo-Chinese style commercial space, "Dong Yun Soft Decoration Organization" focuses on the design and implementation of Neo-Chinese style soft decoration.

CZDF inherits the Eastern classics, leading cultural rejuvenation and integrating the essence of different cultures and times while interpreting the Oriental temperament.

BOKING Art

BOKING Art Studio is a group of persistent artists. Studio's research direction is the unique platinum crystal transparent material as the core to original artistic creation. After years of independent research and development, BOKING wins a major technological breakthrough in the field of materials with its high transparent material molding process. The spirit of perseverance promotes them to continue to break through the limit and create a miracle repeatedly.

Daijie Wu, founder of the studio, considers that contemporary art of China needs innovation, but more in need of historical heritage. Ideal works of art should have sufficient visual beauty to show the existence of human beings as well as a certain philosophical thinking and inspirations.

These pure and bright works are different from today's parrot art form. Whether the theme or style of the work is showing a very unique form of pure personality.

It is commendable that the studio has been in the pursuit of self-character and has been devoted in their work around the same material and technology. This kind of material is transparent as crystals, which can be made in various shapes. BOKING is very fascinated by the material.

DI GAO MEI JU

As a model of luxury home furnishing — DI GAO MEI JU not only inherits the classic charm of Chinese and foreign classical home accessories in design, but also provides products perfectly in match with fashionable jewelry trend, making classical and modern, art and practice perfect unity. The main products of DI GAO MEI JU include high-grade European and American classical ceramics, luxury copper with porcelain home accessories and exquisite hand-painted decorative small furniture. Products bring European and American luxury jewelry a new trend with rare top-quality material and superb craftsmanship. And extensive use of precious metals such as gold, silver, copper and superior porcelain creates a magnificent luxury expression for the jewelry industry. And by increasing the sense of history, in addition to appreciation it also has maintenance, collection and other value.

DI GAO MEI JU shows retro and classic vividly. With elegant shape, exquisite sculpture, European-style modeling, every product is like a piece of artwork, and a feast to the eyes for all people.

FLOLENCO

FLOLENCO Group is a high-end overall home products supplier focusing on the design, production, sale and display of home furnishing products. The brand "FLOLENCO" has been advocating low-key, elegant, tasteful and natural overseas home culture for many years. The company has built up a highly personalized and international art life space for clients, and won many domestic awards and high popularity in home furnishing industry. Professional international design team shuttles every year in Paris, Milan, High Point (North Carolina) and other world's major home furniture exhibitions to collect the latest and most cutting-edge trend of home furnishing. In October 2014, the official opening of the Indian branch, helps to process a new level for the global integration of FLOLENCO boutique home furnishing. In the future FLOLENCO will continue to follow the core values of "sincerity", "quality" and "innovation" and make continuous efforts to create an internationalized home furnishing culture atmosphere and further spread brand culture and fine art life space.

CONTRIBUTORS

Yan Xichao

Mr. Yan advocates the discovery of beautiful things from life. A plant, a building, a piece of jewelry, clothing, and so on, are the source of inspiration, extending his intricate design. Since the creation of Omenia in 2005, he has always been committed to the development of soft ornaments in China.

Mr. Yan brings for soft-decoration design, hotel engineering and other fields a novel fashion light luxury experience since entering the metal home furnishing industry. Diversified style design, emphasizing the balance between personality and practical, applies the forefront of fashion metal jewelry to various fields. His design is the integration of modern urban life attitude and manner, the perfect combination of fashion and furnishings.

Zhang Jun

Zhang Jun, born in Anhui Province in 1976, is major in Chinese classical garden, interior decoration and furniture design. He is an executive vice-chairman of Shenzhen Industry Design Association and executive chairman of Shenzhen Home Furnishing Design Committee. He has led industry innovation with design to promote the development of the industry. In 2014, he was invited to be a visiting professor of Central South University of Forestry and Technology. He is committed to bringing new ideas and frontline experience to students and promoting the development of China's furniture industry. In 2003 and 2011, he created the extension of Top Design and the original modern oriental home furnishing brand — Ease Workshop.

General Manager of Shenzhen Top Design Furniture Co., Ltd;
Vice-chairman of Shenzhen Industry Design Association;
Chairman of Shenzhen Furnishing Design Association;
Deputy Director of the Designers Professional Committee of Shenzhen Furniture Industry Association;
China Furniture top ten professional managers.

ARTPOWER

Acknowledgements

We would like to thank all the designers and companies who made significant contributions to the compilation of this book. Without them, this project would not have been possible. We would also like to thank many others whose names did not appear on the credits, but made specific input and support for the project from beginning to end.

Future Editions

If you would like to contribute to the next edition of Artpower, please email us your details to: artpower@artpower.com.cn